My Country
Great Britain

Cath Senker

FRANKLIN WATTS
LONDON•SYDNEY

First published in 2012
by Franklin Watts

Copyright © Franklin Watts 2012

Franklin Watts
338 Euston Road
London NW1 3BH

Franklin Watts Australia
Level 17/207 Kent Street
Sydney, NSW 2000

Dewey number: 941'.08612
ISBN: 978 1 4451 1048 6

Printed in China

Series Editor: Paul Rockett
Series Designer: Paul Cherrill
  for Basement68
Picture Researcher: Diana Morris

Franklin Watts is a division of
Hachette Children's Books,
an Hachette UK company.

www.hachette.co.uk

Contents

All words in **bold** appear in the glossary on page 23.

 Great Britain in the world

Hi! My name is Jake and I come from Great Britain.

Great Britain is an island in Western Europe. It is a medium-sized country, made up of England, Wales and Scotland.

SCOTLAND

Edinburgh •

Manchester •

WALES

Cardiff •

ENGLAND

• London

Great Britain's place in the world.

4

Great Britain is one of the world's richest countries.

I live in Manchester, a big, important city in the north of England. We have two famous football teams.

Popular football team, Manchester United playing in red and white at their football stadium, Old Trafford.

People who live in Great Britain

A mix of British people at a London market.

Around 63 million people live in Great Britain. People from all over the world have made it their home.

Many come from the Caribbean, India, Pakistan and other countries.

Most people in Great Britain live in cities. The biggest city is the **capital**, London. It has more than 8 million people!

Nearly half of us live near the **coast**. Some people live in the countryside.

In the countryside, walking and cycling are popular.

My grandparents came to Great Britain from Ireland.

What Great Britain looks like

Much of the **landscape** is hilly with low mountains. In the east and south-east the land is flat. Around the long **coastline** are many beaches.

Scotland has many mountains, and it often snows in winter.

The countryside is covered in farmland. Around one-quarter of the land is used for farming.

Big cities like Manchester are packed with busy roads, homes, shops and offices. Our cities also have plenty of parks.

East Anglia, in eastern England, is flat and good for growing crops.

At home with my family

There are all kinds of families in Great Britain. Many children live with both parents. Some live with one parent or have a **stepfamily**.

Many families love playing electronic games.

We mostly enjoy entertainment at home, such as watching TV and playing on computers.

We also like to get together with grandparents, aunts, uncles and cousins.

I like going shopping with my family.

What we eat

In Great Britain, we like to eat meat, potatoes and vegetables, fish and chips, pies and sandwiches. We are fond of fast food, such as burgers and pizza.

People like eating fish and chips covered in salt and vinegar.

We have a choice of food from all over the world! British people adore curries, an Indian dish.

British people are also keen on sweet foods. We love cakes, biscuits and chocolate.

This family are buying a take-away meal to eat at home.

My favourite treat is chocolate cake. What's yours?

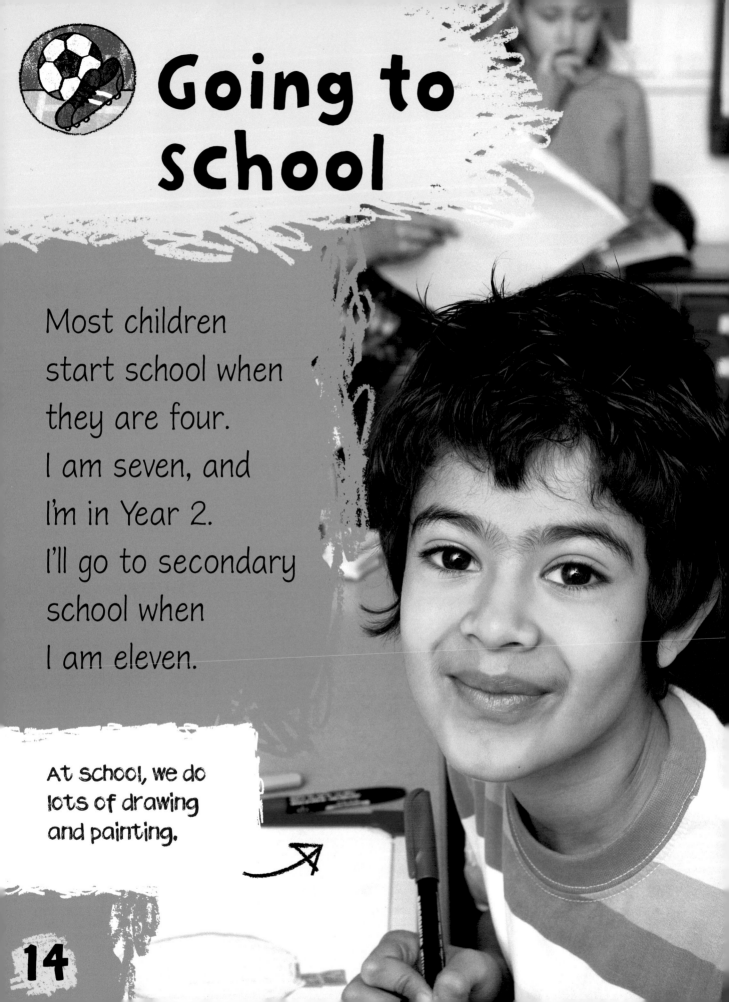

Going to school

Most children start school when they are four. I am seven, and I'm in Year 2. I'll go to secondary school when I am eleven.

At school, we do lots of drawing and painting.

The school day starts
at 9am. We have a short
lunch break. We all eat
our lunch at school.
Home time is 3pm.

Most children eat
school dinners,
but some bring a
packed lunch.

At 3pm I go to
after-school club until my
parents finish work
and pick me up.

Festivals and celebrations

christmas is a christian festival, but everyone enjoys the holiday.

Our main **festival** is Christmas on 25 December. New Year on 1 January is a big holiday too.

In Scotland especially, people celebrate **New Year's Eve** with street parties and music.

On 5 November, people light bonfires and fireworks to celebrate **Bonfire Night.**

People of different religions celebrate their own festivals. For example, Muslims hold a delicious feast to celebrate **Eid ul-Fitr.**

Firework displays light up the sky on Bonfire Night.

19

Things to see

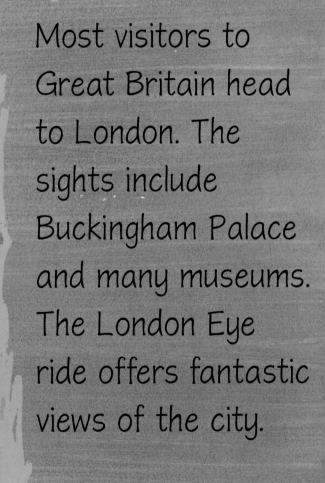

Most visitors to Great Britain head to London. The sights include Buckingham Palace and many museums. The London Eye ride offers fantastic views of the city.

On the London Eye you can see as far as 40km on a clear day!

Edinburgh, Manchester, Birmingham and Cardiff have many sights too.

Across the country are zoos, theme parks and castles. You can go on lovely walks around lakes and forests and climb hills.

Edinburgh castle in Scotland attracts thousands of visitors.

I love visiting castles, although they can be creepy.

Index